Isle of Man
Tax Saving Guide

2011/12

By Nick Braun PhD

Important Legal Notices:

Taxcafe®
Tax Guide - "Isle of Man Tax Saving Guide"

Published by:
Taxcafe UK Limited
67 Milton Road
Kirkcaldy KY1 1TL
Tel: (0044) 01592 560081
Email: team@taxcafe.co.uk

First edition, April 2011

ISBN 978-1-907302-47-3

Trademarks
Taxcafe® is a registered trademark of Taxcafe UK Limited. All other logos, trademarks, names and logos in this tax guide may be trademarks of their respective owners.

Disclaimer
Before reading or relying on the content of this tax guide please read the disclaimer carefully. If you have any queries then please contact the publisher at team@taxcafe.co.uk.

Disclaimer

1. Please note that this publication is intended as general guidance only and does NOT constitute accountancy, tax, financial or other professional advice. The author and Taxcafe UK Limited make no representations or warranties with respect to the accuracy or completeness of the contents of this publication and cannot accept any responsibility for any liability, loss or risk, personal or otherwise, which may arise, directly or indirectly, from reliance on information contained in this publication.

2. Please note that tax legislation, the law and practices of governments and regulatory authorities are constantly changing. Furthermore, your personal circumstances may vary from the general information contained in this guide which may not be suitable for your situation. We therefore recommend that for accountancy, tax, financial or other professional advice, you consult a suitably qualified accountant, tax specialist, independent financial adviser, or other professional adviser. Your professional adviser will be able to provide specific advice based on your personal circumstances.

3. All persons described in the examples in this book are entirely fictional characters created specifically for the purposes of this guide. Any similarities to actual persons, living or dead, or to fictional characters created by any other author, are entirely coincidental.

About the Author & Taxcafe

Nick Braun founded Taxcafe in Edinburgh in 1999 along with his partner, Aileen Smith. As the driving force behind the company, their aim is to provide affordable plain-English tax information for private individuals and investors, business owners, IFAs and accountants.

Since then Taxcafe has become one of the best-known tax publishers in the UK and won several business awards.

Nick has been involved in the tax publishing world since 1989 as a writer, editor and publisher. He holds a masters degree and PhD in economics from the University of Glasgow, where he was awarded the prestigious William Glen Scholarship and later became a Research Fellow.

Prior to that he graduated with distinction from the University of South Africa, the country's oldest university, earning the highest economics results in the university's history. He went on to become editor of *Personal Finance* and *Tax Breaks*, two of South Africa's best-known financial publications, before moving to the UK in 1994.

Nick is also an Enrolled Agent, a tax professional recognized by the United States federal government to represent taxpayers in dealings with the Internal Revenue Service (IRS).

When he's not working, Nick likes to spend time with his children and eat good food!

Dedication

Once again, to Aileen for all your love and support and to Jake,
Sandy and Tilly for all the joy you bring.

Contents

Introduction

The Isle of Man does not have the lowest income tax rates in the world. Monaco and the Cayman Islands, for example, have no taxes at all. However, paying some tax is the price you pay to live in a tax haven situated no more than one hour from the British mainland, with the same culture and lifestyle.

Furthermore, some of the most hated taxes in Britain do not even exist on the Isle of Man, including:

- Capital Gains Tax
- Inheritance Tax
- Stamp Duty Land Tax

There is also no wealth tax or gift tax.

Unlike many tax havens, which make it difficult if not impossible for anyone except the ultra rich to obtain residence, the Isle of Man welcomes entrepreneurs and you may even qualify for some free cash from the Manx Government (see Chapter 10).

If you are a British citizen you do not require permission from the Isle of Man Immigration Office to live on the island.

However, if you want to get a job there (or take up self-employment) you may require a work permit issued under the Isle of Man Control of Employment Acts.

Similar rules apply to Irish citizens and European Economic Area (EEA) nationals.

Tax Years

Individuals and trusts are taxed by reference to the tax year, which, like the UK, runs from 6th April to the following 5th April. Returns should be filed by 6th October.

Companies are taxed on an accounting year basis. Returns should be filed within 12 months and one day of the year-end. Any tax due is also payable by this time.

2

Chapter 1

Key Facts about the Isle of Man

Geography and Climate

The Isle of Man is located in the middle of the Irish Sea, 83 miles from Liverpool and 90 miles from Belfast.

The island is 33 miles long from north to south and 14 miles wide from east to west. The capital is Douglas, situated on the east coast. Other towns include Port Erin, Port St Mary, Peel and Ramsey.

The Isle of Man enjoys a climate similar to many parts of the UK. Summers are cool with clear skies. The average summer temperature is in the early to mid 20 degrees centigrade, with the temperature at night hovering around 10 degrees.

Winters are mild and wet with an average temperature of around nine degrees. There is less rainfall in the north and south of the island but plenty in the hilly interior, especially on Snaefell, the island's only mountain, standing at 2036 feet.

There is rarely any frost or snow on the Isle of Man and the island does not experience overcast skies as much as other parts of the UK – strong winds keep the clouds moving!

A thick sea fog occasionally covers the lowland areas and is known locally as Manannan's Cloak – a reference to a mythical shroud that the ancient sea god Manannan would throw over the island to protect it from enemies.

Government

The Isle of Man is a self-governing British Crown Dependency. It is not part of the United Kingdom, although the Queen is the sovereign.

The Manx Parliament, Tynwald, legislates on domestic matters but responsibility for defence and foreign affairs has been left with the British Government.

Tynwald consists of two houses:

- The House of Keys is the lower house and consists of 24 members, elected for five-year terms.
- The Legislative Council is the upper house and consists of eight politicians from the House of Keys plus the Lord Bishop and the Attorney General.

The House of Keys typically initiates legislation. The Legislative Council recommends amendments that are referred back to the House of Keys for review.

Day-to-day government matters are administered by Tynwald departments, each of which has a minister.

The cabinet consists of nine ministers. The Chief Minister is the nearest equivalent to a prime minister.

Legal System

The Isle of Man has its own independent legal system, based on English common law.

High Court judges are called Deemsters and have jurisdiction over all civil and criminal matters. The court of appeal is known as the Staff of Government Division and consists of a Deemster and the Judge of Appeal.

The Judicial Committee of the Privy Council is the court of final appeal.

Population and Language

The Isle of Man has a population of just over 80,000. This equates to approximately 360 people per square mile. One-third of the population live in Douglas.

Roughly half the inhabitants were born on the island and the rest are mainly British, although there are people from many other countries working in the financial industry and other sectors.

Economy

The Isle of Man is best known as an international offshore financial centre with low tax rates. In recent years the Government has encouraged diversification into other sectors including online gambling, films, aircraft and ship registration, and high-tech manufacturing. There is even an established sector conducting space-related activities.

Other key facts about the economy:

- The unit of currency on the island is the British pound.
- Unemployment is 2%
- Inflation is 6.7%
- GDP per capita is US$35,000 (almost identical to the UK).

Obtaining Permission to Live in the Isle of Man

If you are a British citizen you do not require permission from the Isle of Man Immigration Office to live on the island. However, if you want to work (or take up self-employment) there you may require a work permit issued under the Isle of Man Control of Employment Acts. Similar rules apply to Irish citizens and European Economic Area (EEA) nationals.

For more info go to:
www.gov.im/ded/employmentrights/workpermits.xml

Travelling to the Isle of Man

You can travel to the island either by sea or air. A number of airlines serve the Isle of Man and a full list of flights can be found at the Isle of Man airport website: www.iom-airport.com

Flying times are:

- One hour from:

    o Bristol
    o Gloucester Airport
    o Newcastle
    o London (with flights leaving from Gatwick, Luton and City Airport)

- 45 minutes from:

    o Manchester
    o Birmingham
    o Leeds

- 30 minutes from:

    o Dublin
    o Liverpool

- 20 minutes from:

    o Belfast

Flybe (www.flybe.com) flies to the Isle of Man from most major UK cities. At the time of writing, ticket costs vary from £30 to £80 each way (including taxes), depending on what day you travel and how far in advance you book.

Ferries are available from Liverpool, Heysham (Lancaster), Belfast and Dublin and can take from two hours 30 minutes on the fast craft or three hours 30 minutes on the conventional ferry. Routes are operated by the Isle of Man Steam Packet company.

Chapter 2

How to Become an Isle of Man Resident for Tax Purposes

Isle of Man Resident

Isle of Man residents are taxed on their worldwide income.

There is no definition of residence in the Isle of Man tax legislation. If you move to the island with the intention of living there permanently or for at least a complete tax year, you will normally be considered to be resident from the date you arrive.

In terms of a 2007 practice note issued by the Isle of Man Income Tax Division, you will be treated as a resident for tax purposes if:

- You are present on the island for more than six months during any tax year, or

- Your visits average 91 days or more over a four-year period (not counting days of arrival and departure). You will then be resident in the fifth year.

A Word of Warning for UK Residents

The newspapers often tease us with stories of rich and famous actors and sports stars who live in glamorous tax havens like Monaco or the Bahamas.

With the UK's top income tax and national insurance rate having risen to 52% in April 2011, many taxpayers may be considering moving abroad to escape High Tax Britain.

A non-resident may be able to avoid both UK income tax and capital gains tax. The problem is that nobody seems to know how to become one! The term 'non-resident' has never been defined in the UK tax legislation.

It used to be thought that to become non-resident, all you had to do was leave the country and limit your visits to the UK to less than 91 days per year on average (and less than 183 days in any single tax year).

It turns out that the number of days you spend in the UK is just one of the factors HMRC will look at when determining your residence status.

Nowadays you have to show that you have made a 'distinct break' from the UK and severed many of your ties to the country. Unfortunately this is an extremely subjective test.

As a result, many expats can no longer be absolutely certain that they are in fact non-resident, even though they have lived abroad for many years.

Before we explain how HMRC determines your residence status, it's important to point out that there is one type of individual who will probably still find it relatively easy to become non-resident.

Working Abroad

If you go abroad to work full time you will become non-resident, without having to sever your ties to the UK, provided:

- You are leaving to work abroad under a contract of employment for at least one whole tax year;

- You have actually left the UK to begin your employment abroad and not to have a holiday before you begin your employment;

- You will be absent from the UK for at least a whole tax year; and

- Your return visits total less than 183 days in any tax year, and average less than 91 days per tax year on a four-year average.

Under these circumstances, you will become non-resident for income tax purposes from the day after the day of your departure.

(You will not become non-resident for capital gains tax purposes until at least the start of the next tax year.)

Your spouse will also enjoy the same tax treatment, even if not in full-time employment abroad, provided he or she lives abroad for at least a whole tax year and meets the 183 day and 91 day tests.

Leaving the UK Permanently

If you do not leave the UK to work in full-time employment, you can become non-resident by demonstrating to HMRC that you have left the UK permanently or indefinitely.

According to HMRC guidance:

"Leaving the UK 'permanently' means that you are leaving the country to live abroad and will not return here to live. Leaving 'indefinitely' means that you are leaving to live abroad for a long time (at least three years) but you think that you might eventually return to live here, although you do not currently have plans to do so."

Apart from leaving the country you must also make a definite break from the UK and sever many of your social and economic ties.

How to Sever Ties with the UK

The following are some (but not all) of the factors HMRC will look at when building a picture about your ties to the UK:

- Family ties – do your spouse, children or other family members live in the UK?

- Social ties – do you have club memberships or regularly attend events?

- Business ties – are you a director of a UK company? Do you have employment or self-employment in the UK? Do you have regular employment duties in the UK? Do you repeatedly come to the UK for business meetings?

- Property ties – do you own a property in the UK? Do you own a rental property that also provides you with accommodation when you visit the UK?

Some ties are easier to sever than others. Selling your UK home and making sure that you do not have available accommodation in the UK is very important and arguably one of the easier things you can do.

Clearly, some emigrants will find it easier than others to convince the taxman that they are non-resident.

Those who leave the country, sell all their UK assets, take their families with them, set up a new business or start a new job in their new homeland, only returning very occasionally (for example for a couple of weeks every year to visit friends), will probably not find it difficult to convince the taxman that they are non-UK resident.

It seems that HMRC's main grudge is against those who want to have their cake and eat it: by keeping a home and business interests in the UK, while also claiming non-resident status.

One such individual is Robert Gaines-Cooper, whose case goes before the Supreme Court later this year, following his defeat in the Court of Appeal last year. As much as £30 million of tax is at stake.

Gaines-Cooper is a multimillionaire globetrotting businessman with interests in many countries. He insists that he is non-UK resident because he has been based in the Seychelles for the last 30 years and has religiously kept to the taxman's published guidance by spending less than 91 days a year in the UK.

Unfortunately the judges in the Court of Appeal disagreed. They followed the taxman's line that day counting is just one factor that needs to be taken into consideration when determining an individual's residence status.

The judges looked for the 'centre of gravity' of Mr Gaines-Cooper's life and interests and decided that it had remained in the UK.

Gaines-Cooper made many mistakes that could arguably be avoided by anyone wanting to become non-resident: he kept many unnecessary UK ties, he didn't move to a country that had a tax treaty with the UK (a tax treaty could have more easily determined in which country he was resident), he kept a home and car collection in the UK and his wife and child lived in the country.

Many expats won't know where they stand for sure until the final outcome of this case is known.

Possibly the most difficult tie to sever could be your business interests in the UK. Those who retain business interests in the UK face the possibility of having their non-resident status challenged.

Statutory Residence Test

The position may become a little clearer in future, as the Government is hoping to introduce a statutory residence test from April 2012, following a period of consultation.

UK Assets

It's important to remember that, even if you do achieve non-resident status, you will still have to pay UK income tax on certain assets you leave behind. Furthermore, to avoid capital gains tax, you will need to be both non-resident and non-ordinarily resident for at least five complete UK tax years.

UK Properties

For example, if you own rental properties in the UK, you will probably have to pay UK income tax on your rental profits.

I say 'probably' because the tax treatment may depend on the terms of any double tax agreement between the UK and your new country of residence. Most treaties give the UK the right to continue taxing you on property here, however.

So, if you earn all your income from UK rental property, you may not save a penny in tax by fleeing to a tax haven.

By becoming non-resident you will, however, be able to sell your properties and escape UK capital gains tax, provided you remain non-resident for at least five complete UK tax years. You can then start a new property empire elsewhere!

For those with more modest incomes, it is worth noting that UK nationals, EU citizens and certain other individuals who become non-UK resident are still entitled to claim the £7,475 income tax personal allowance.

Couples can therefore enjoy up to £14,950 of UK rental profits without having to worry about UK income tax.

UK Business

If you own a sole trader business or a share of a partnership based in the UK, you will be subject to UK tax on your profits.

If you own a UK company, you generally can't take it with you when you become non-resident. Its profits will usually continue to be subject to UK corporation tax. From April 2011, the tax rate is 20% on the first £300,000 of profits.

The after-tax profits can, however, be extracted by way of a dividend, which could be subject to the income tax rules of your new country of residence.

Chapter 3

Capital Gains Tax and Inheritance Tax

Capital Gains Tax

There is no capital gains tax in the Isle of Man. This means that Isle of Man residents do not pay any tax when they sell investment properties, stock market shares or businesses.

In the UK, capital gains are taxed at 18% if you are a basic-rate taxpayer (generally speaking if you earn less than £42,475 during the current 2011/12 tax year) and 28% if you are a higher-rate taxpayer.

However, only those who expect to earn substantial capital gains will benefit from moving to the Isle of Man to avoid capital gains tax. This is because there are a number of exemptions and reliefs for capital gains made by UK taxpayers:

- The first £10,600 is tax free (£21,200 for couples)
- Up to £10,680 can be invested in tax-free ISAs each year (£21,360 for couples)
- Spread betting profits are tax free
- Entrepreneurs pay just 10% capital gains tax thanks to Entrepreneurs Relief

Furthermore, to avoid capital gains tax, you will need to be both non-resident and non-ordinarily resident for at least five complete UK tax years.

Inheritance Tax

There is no inheritance tax on the Isle of Man.

However, if you retain a UK domicile of origin, UK inheritance tax will apply to your assets worldwide. Furthermore, a UK domiciled individual is deemed to be UK domiciled for three complete tax years after leaving the UK and taking on a domicile of choice elsewhere, ie your worldwide assets will be subject to UK inheritance tax for three tax years after you permanently leave the UK to live in the Isle of Man.

Even if you are non-UK domiciled you will still be subject to UK inheritance tax on any UK assets.

Chapter 4

Income Tax:
Big Savings for UK Taxpayers

Income Tax

Unlike some tax havens, like Monaco or the Bahamas, the Isle of Man does levy income tax. However, income tax rates are almost universally lower in the Isle of Man than in the UK and Manx residents enjoy certain tax concessions that are not available to UK taxpayers (e.g. married couples can be assessed jointly and there is tax relief for mortgage interest).

Income tax is levied as follows:

- The first £9,300   0%
- Next £10,500   10%
- Above £19,800   20%

The 10% rate is known as the standard rate and the 20% rate is known as the higher rate.

(Note: those aged over 65 enjoy an additional £2,020 of tax-free income.)

£115,000 Tax Cap

Very high earners can benefit from a £115,000 tax cap – no matter how high your income, you need never pay more than £115,000 in income tax.

In order to benefit from the tax cap (rather than paying income tax at the above rates) you would need to have income of approximately £590,000 during the current 2011/12 tax year.

The cap does not apply automatically – an application has to be made to the Assessor of Income Tax.

The tax cap is £230,000 for couples assessed jointly but it is possible for husbands and wives to be taxed independently so that one spouse can take advantage of the £115,000 tax cap (e.g. if one spouse's income is much higher than that of the other spouse).

Isle of Man Income Tax vs UK Income Tax

How do Isle of Man income tax rates compare with UK income tax rates?

In the UK income tax is levied as follows:

- The first £7,475   0%
- Next £35,000   20%
- Above £42,475   40%

High income earners in the UK are clobbered by two further tax measures:

- Firstly, anyone with income over £100,000 has their £7,475 income tax personal allowance gradually taken away. £1 of personal allowance is taken away for every £2 you earn over £100,000. For example, if your income is £105,000 your personal allowance will be reduced by £2,500.

- Secondly, income over £150,000 is taxed at 50%.

Sample Income Tax Savings

Some examples of UK and Isle of Man income tax bills are shown in Table 1. These are based on rates for 2011/12.

The final column shows how much income tax you could save by living in the Isle of Man.

Only you can decide whether these tax savings are sufficient to justify moving to the Isle of Man.

However, it's important to point out that these are *annual* tax savings that could be enjoyed every year. For example, someone earning £80,000 will potentially save around £90,000 after 10 years, should the difference in tax rates remain the same.

TABLE 1
Isle of Man vs UK Income Tax 2011/12

Income £	Isle of Man £	UK £	Tax Saving £
15,000	90	1,505	1,415
20,000	1,090	2,505	1,415
30,000	3,090	4,505	1,415
40,000	5,090	6,505	1,415
50,000	7,090	10,010	2,920
60,000	9,090	14,010	4,920
70,000	11,090	18,010	6,920
80,000	13,090	22,010	8,920
90,000	15,090	26,010	10,920
100,000	17,090	30,010	12,920
125,000	22,090	43,000	20,910
150,000	27,090	53,000	25,910
200,000	37,090	78,000	40,910
300,000	57,090	128,000	70,910
500,000	97,090	228,000	130,910
750,000	115,000	353,000	238,000
1 million	115,000	478,000	363,000

Of course, income tax rates can and do change and over time the Isle of Man tax regime could become less generous and the UK tax regime could become more generous (for example, the 50% income tax rate is widely expected to be abolished in 2013).

Married Couples

Another tax benefit of living in the Isle of Man is that married couples can elect to be taxed jointly, which results in a doubling up of the £9,300 tax-free allowance and 10% standard rate tax band.

Married couples are not automatically taxed in this way. Those who do not apply for joint assessment are taxed separately.

Married couples assessed jointly are therefore taxed as follows:

- The first £18,600   0%
- Next £21,000   10%
- Above £39,600   20%

Who benefits from joint assessment?

In the UK it is relatively easy for married couples to share ownership of assets that produce taxable income, e.g. rental properties, share portfolios and bank accounts. It is also possible in many circumstances to share the ownership of private companies, with both spouses taking a share of any dividends declared.

Splitting income in this way allows some married couples in the UK (e.g. where one spouse doesn't work or has a relatively low income) to make full use of two income tax personal allowances and two basic-rate tax bands.

However, not all income can be split for tax purposes. In particular, someone who earns a big salary and pays tax at 40% or 50% cannot split this income with their spouse so that some of the income is taxed at 20%. Many sole traders will also struggle to split their business profits with their spouses.

In the Isle of Man the situation is completely different: all income can be assessed jointly.

Example

Jack earns a salary of £100,000. His wife Jill does not work and has no taxable income. The couple decide to be assessed jointly. As a result income tax is payable as follows on Jack's salary:

- *The first £18,600   0%*
- *Next £21,000   10%*
- *Final £60,400   20%*

With joint assessment the couple's tax bill is £14,180. If the couple were assessed separately Jack would pay income tax of £17,090 – an increase of £2,910 per year.

How much is this tax concession worth?

Because married couples can enjoy an additional £9,300 of income taxed at 0% (instead of 20%) and an additional £10,500 taxed at 10% (instead of 20%), this means married couples in the Isle of Man can save up to an additional £2,910 in income tax every year.

Mortgage Interest

Here's a tax relief that may make you nostalgic. Many years ago it was possible for UK taxpayers to obtain mortgage interest tax relief (MIRAS) on their homes.

Isle of Man residents can still claim this tax relief, although the amount you can claim has been reduced significantly in recent years.

For the current 2011/12 tax year mortgage and loan interest paid to an Isle of Man lender is tax deductible up to £7,500 (£15,000 for married couples taxed jointly).

This means that Jack and Jill in the above example can reduce their taxable income by up to £15,000 in the current tax year. This could save them an additional £3,000 in income tax:

$$£15,000 \times 20\% = £3,000$$

Educational Deeds of Covenant

Up until 5th April 2011 it was possible for parents or grandparents to enter into an 'Educational Deed of Covenant' (EDC) with their children or grandchildren.

A payment of up to £5,500 per year could be paid to each child in higher education. Such amounts were tax deductible in the hands of the person making the payment and taxable in the hands of the student (but effectively tax free as they would be covered by the income tax personal allowance).

Tax relief will continue for EDCs entered into on or before 5th April 2011. Tax relief for new EDCs has now been abolished.

Charitable Donations

Charitable donations of up to £7,000 per person are tax deductible.

Pension Contributions

Isle of Man residents can make pension contributions and enjoy income tax relief. The basic rules for pension contributions are as follows:

- The maximum pension contribution is £300,000 per year
- Income tax relief is limited to the lower of £300,000 and 100% of your relevant earnings
- Like in the UK, non-earners can contribute up to £3,600

Other pension rules are as follows:

- The maximum tax-free lump sum is 30%
- There is no mandatory purchase of an annuity
- Funds remaining on death are taxed at 7.5% when paid out to beneficiaries

UK Pensions

In terms of the Double Tax Agreement between the UK and the Isle of Man it is possible for an Isle of Man resident to receive a UK pension without any UK income tax deducted.

In some cases the entire pension plan can be transferred to the Isle of Man and subject to Isle of Man Qualifying Recognised Overseas Pension Scheme (QROPS) rules, which may be more flexible than the rules governing UK pension schemes.

Benefits in Kind

Most benefits in kind (non-cash salary payments) are taxed but there are some useful exemptions.

For starters, there is a general tax exemption where the total value of benefits is less than £400 (this applies to benefits in kind other than company cars and company car fuel).

The aggregation is based on £400 per employee per employer.

Exempt Benefits

Other benefits in kind that can be provided tax free to employees include:

- Approved profit sharing or savings-related share option schemes
- Broadband connection
- Car parking fees used principally for business purposes
- Christmas party expenses up to £100 per head
- Commercial vehicles such as a van or a lorry where the main business purpose is the transportation of goods and materials.
- Electric cars - does not include hybrid petrol electric cars
- Meals in a works canteen
- Medical insurance, dental insurance and health screening for employees provided by an employer's scheme
- Mobile telephone, where contract is in the name of the employer
- Nursery or crèche facilities directly paid to a registered child minding facility, by the employer, on behalf of an employee
- General benefits that do not exceed £400 per annum
- Personal computer and computer devices that do not exceed the aggregate cash equivalent of £1000
- Plant and machinery where used for business purposes
- Provision of a scheme to provide benefits to employees or dependants on retirement or death
- Public transport season tickets or multi-journey tickets provided by the employer
- Safety work clothing such as hard hats, high-visibility jackets and safety boots
- Sports and recreational facilities at an employer's place of work

Taxable Benefits

The following benefits are taxable:

- Accommodation, free or subsidised
- Board and lodgings provided
- Clothing other than uniform
- Dental cover for non-employees
- Domestic staff provided
- Fuel provided
- Gift vouchers
- Goods or services provided by an employer
- Heat and light provided or payment of personal bills such as rates, satellite TV, insurance
- Long-service awards with a value of over £400
- Meals
- Medical cover for non employees
- Membership of gym, golf club etc.
- Motor vehicle and fuel provided
- Property below market value
- Shares granted under unapproved schemes
- Transfer of ownership of company asset to employee

Company Cars

If an employer provides an employee with a company car in the Isle of Man there will be a taxable benefit in kind charge.

The benefit in kind charge is based on the car's cylinder capacity:

Cylinder capacity	Car rate (£)	Fuel rate (£)
Electric cars	Nil	Nil
1000 or less	800	800
1001-1200	1,100	950
1201-1800	3,600	1,500
1801-2500	5,000	1,750
2501-3500	7,000	2,000
3501-5000	10,000	2,250
More than 5000	12,000	2,500

Chapter 5

National Insurance

One tax you may not be able to escape by moving to the Isle of Man is national insurance. National insurance rates in the Isle of Man are quite similar to those levied in the UK.

The 1% increase to UK national insurance rates that came into effect in April 2011 was not implemented in the Isle of Man. That's the good news. The bad news is that national insurance kicks in at a lower level of income than in the UK.

Fortunately, national insurance is only levied on *earned* income. So retirees and those who live off investment income (e.g. dividends, rental income and interest) do not have to worry about this additional tax.

Because dividends are not subject to national insurance, many company owners are able to avoid national insurance on their own income by taking dividends instead of salary.

However, if you set up a business in the Isle of Man and employ people, you will still have to pay 12.8% national insurance on a big chunk of your employees' income – a potentially significant tax cost for a country that is supposed to be a tax haven!

Isle of Man vs UK National Insurance

Employees

For the current 2011/12 tax year, employees pay national insurance as follows:

Isle of Man			UK		
On the first	£5,980	0%	On the first	£7,225	0%
On the next	£33,020	11%	On the next	£35,250	12%
Above	£39,000	1%	Above	£42,475	2%

In the Isle of Man employers pay 12.8% on all income over £5,980.

In the UK employers pay 13.8% on all income over £7,075.

Table 2 compares Isle of Man and UK national insurance bills for different salaries. Generally Isle of Man tax bills are lower (possibly by thousands of pounds) but for those on very low salaries the Isle of Man national insurance bill is higher.

TABLE 2
Isle of Man vs UK National Insurance 2011/12

	Isle of Man			UK		
Income	Employee	Employer	Total	Employee	Employer	Total
£	£	£	£	£	£	£
15,000	992	1,155	2,147	933	1,094	2,027
20,000	1,542	1,795	3,337	1,533	1,784	3,317
30,000	2,642	3,075	5,717	2,733	3,164	5,897
40,000	3,642	4,355	7,997	3,933	4,544	8,477
50,000	3,742	5,635	9,377	4,381	5,924	10,304
60,000	3,842	6,915	10,757	4,581	7,304	11,884
70,000	3,942	8,195	12,137	4,781	8,684	13,464
80,000	4,042	9,475	13,517	4,981	10,064	15,044
90,000	4,142	10,755	14,897	5,181	11,444	16,624
100,000	4,242	12,035	16,277	5,381	12,824	18,204
125,000	4,492	15,235	19,727	5,881	16,274	22,154
150,000	4,742	18,435	23,177	6,381	19,724	26,104
200,000	5,242	24,835	30,077	7,381	26,624	34,004
300,000	6,242	37,635	43,877	9,381	40,424	49,804
500,000	8,242	63,235	71,477	13,381	68,024	81,404
750,000	10,742	95,235	105,977	18,381	102,524	120,904

Self Employed

For the current 2011/12 tax year, self-employed individuals (sole traders and partnerships) pay national insurance as follows:

Isle of Man			**UK**		
On the first	£5,980	0%	On the first	£7,225	0%
On the next	£33,020	8%	On the next	£35,250	9%
Above	£39,000	1%	Above	£42,475	2%

In both countries there is an additional £130 in class 2 contributions for anyone with profits over £5,315.

Chapter 6

VAT

Not much to say about this tax!

VAT is levied at 20% and the VAT rules are pretty much identical to those operating in the UK.

The UK and Isle of Man form a common area for the purposes of VAT and customs duties.

The VAT registration limit is £70,000; the deregistration limit is £68,000.

Chapter 7

Company Tax

The Corporate Income Tax rate for most Isle of Man companies is 0%. That's right –Manx companies can pay zero taxes on their profits.

This is one of the major attractions of running a business out of the Isle of Man.

How does this compare with the tax position of UK companies? For the current financial year UK companies pay corporation tax as follows:

Tax Payable by UK Companies 1st April 2011 to 31st March 2012	
On the first £300,000 profits	20%
On profits between £300,000 and £1.5 million	27.5%
On profits over £1.5 million	26%

Not all companies in the Isle of Man pay 0%. A 10% rate of tax applies to income received by a company from any of the following sources:

- Banking business
- Land and property in the Isle of Man (including property development, residential and commercial rental or property letting and mining and quarrying).

Attribution Regime for Individuals (ARI)

At present, where a company has Isle of Man resident shareholders, a piece of anti-avoidance legislation called the Attribution Regime for Individuals (ARI) applies.

31

This tax measure is designed to stop Isle of Man company owners from rolling up income tax free inside their companies.

This is how it works:

If a dividend of 55% or more of the distributable profits is NOT paid within 12 months of the end of the company's accounting period, the company becomes 'relevant'. This means that 100% of the company's distributable profits will be taxed in the hands of the Isle of Man resident shareholders.

When it comes to investment companies (companies that derive more than 50% of their total income from investment, eg rental properties), 100% of the distributable profits are taxable in the hands of Manx resident shareholders, in proportion to their shareholding.

Good News in the 2011 Budget

In the 2011 Budget it was announced that the Attribution Regime for Individuals will be abolished for accounting periods beginning from 6th April 2012.

This is because the tax anti-avoidance measure was set to be declared harmful under the EU Code of Conduct for Business Taxation because it penalises Manx resident shareholders.

On the face of it, this means that in future, shareholders of Isle of Man companies may be able to roll up the profits in their companies free of tax. We will have to wait and see what, if any, changes are made to the corporate tax system in the months ahead.

Dividend Income

Companies do not pay tax on dividends received from other Isle of Man resident companies and dividends received from non-resident companies are taxed at 0%.

Business Structures

The Isle of Man has a number of different types of business organisations. The most commonly used are:

- 1931 Act Limited Company
- 2006 Act Company
- Protected Cell Company (PCC)
- Foreign Company (F Registered)
- Limited Liability Company (LLC)
- Partnerships
- Limited Partnerships
- Trusts

The Companies Act 2006 introduced a simplified type of company on to the Isle of Man business scene and swept away some of the corporate red tape, including the concept of authorised share capital and the requirements to hold annual general meetings, appoint a company secretary, and filing requirements.

A protected cell company is a company that separates the assets and liabilities of different classes/series of shares from each other. Essentially a PCC allows you to have lots of companies inside one company, thereby increasing the legal liability protection.

The limited liability company is one of the most popular business structures in the United States. Like companies, LLCs offer liability protection but are taxed like partnerships.

Chapter 8

Capital Allowances

Cars

For tax purposes you can claim a tax deduction of 25% of the written-down value of the car each year (up to a maximum of £3000 per year). This is known as a writing-down allowance.

Example

Year 1	Motor car bought for	£14,000
	Writing-down allowance 25% (restricted to £3,000 maximum)	£3,000
	Written-down value carried forward	£11,000
Year 2	Written-down value brought forward	£11,000
	Writing-down allowance (25% no restriction)	£2,750
	Written-down value carried forward	£8,250

Plant & Machinery

For tax purposes you can write down up to 100% of the value of equipment, machinery and vans by claiming what is known as a First Year Allowance.

If you decide to claim less than 100% in the first year, a writing-down allowance of up to 25% can be claimed on the balance in future years.

Example

Year 1	Van bought for	£14,000
	First year allowance claimed (50%)	£7,000
	Written-down value carried forward	£7,000
Year 2	Written-down value brought forward	£7,000
	Writing-down allowance (25%)	£1,750
	Written-down value carried forward	£5,250

Buildings

Industrial buildings:
First-year allowance   100%
Writing-down allowance   4%

Tourist premises:
First-year allowance   100%
Writing-down allowance   10%

Agricultural buildings:
First-year allowance   100%
Writing-down allowance   10%

Chapter 9

International Tax Agreements

The Isle of Man Treasury has entered into a wide variety of tax treaties and is in active negotiations to conclude taxation agreements with Canada, Italy, The Netherlands and Spain.

The Isle of Man has entered into four Double Taxation Agreements with the following countries:

- Belgium
- Estonia
- Malta
- United Kingdom

The Isle of Man has entered into 17 Tax Information Exchange Agreements with the following countries:

- Australia
- Denmark
- Faroe Islands
- Finland
- France
- Germany
- Greenland
- Iceland
- Ireland
- Netherlands
- New Zealand
- Norway
- Portugal
- Sweden
- United Kingdom
- China
- US

Chapter 10

Business Grants

Financial Assistance Scheme

The Isle of Man Government is extremely keen to bring entrepreneurs to the island.

To this end the Department of Economic Development's Financial Assistance Scheme (FAS) provides grants and soft loans.

The kind of company that will qualify for a grant is one that has good growth prospects and will provide a long-term economic benefit for the island, for example increased employment.

It is possible to obtain grant approval before relocating to the island.

Available assistance includes:

Capital Grants

- Up to 40% of cost of new buildings, building improvements, new plant and machinery, including hardware and software

Operating Grants

- Up to 40% of non-recurring costs associated with the establishment of a project

- Up to 40% of the costs of specific new marketing ventures

- Up to 40% of the costs of implementing quality standards, energy conservation etc

- Up to 40% of the cost of renting a factory from a private developer for the initial period of a new project

Training grants are considered but must relate to a project to which financial assistance is being given.

The above incentives apply to existing and new ventures and can be applied for on an annual basis.

An e-business could expect between 20% and 40% support.

For more information visit:
www.gov.im/ded/grants/financeassist.xml

Business Support Scheme

The Business Support Scheme offers a grant of 50% towards the cost of getting expert business advice (and possibly new software) up to £4,500 per project.

For more information: www.gov.im/ded/grants/bss

Small Business Start-Up Scheme

This scheme offers two financial incentives:

- Up to £1,500 for materials and equipment for your business. This is matched spending – ie you spend £1,500 and the Manx Government will spend £1,500.

- A living allowance of £50 per week for 30 weeks.

You will also receive advice from a business adviser for 18 months.

For more information: www.gov.im/ded/training/SBSU